Shoreham
Past and Presen

CU00686893

New & Revised Edition

Joy Saynor and Garry Weaser

Shoreham & District Historical Society

Dedicated to our Founder Chairman
Dr William Lothian MB ChB

ISBN   978-0-9539543-3-9

Published by
Shoreham & District Historical Society
Lynda Alleeson, Secretary, Shoreham Kent • www.shorehamkenthistorical.org.uk

Typeset & Printed by
Silver Pines Services, Pinewood Avenue, Sevenoaks TN14 5AF • www.silverpines.co.uk

Shoreham Past and Present

Introduction

This small study, contrasting the recent past of Shoreham with the present, was first published in 2000 by the Shoreham and District Historical Society to commemorate the millennium year. It aimed, as does this new publication, to contrast varying scenes of the village at a time when maps, watercolours, drawings and photographs were becoming widely available with the same views at the present day. Some well-known scenes have had to be omitted where no early record has survived. The Historical Society sponsored and encouraged the research for the first edition and grateful acknowledgement must be given to the Shoreham Society and to the Allen Grove Fund of the Kent Archaeological Society for their assistance at that time.

The greatest general change for the village in the last two hundred years has been the loss of its isolation: in the past, it was remote from the metropolis, had bad roads and an unnavigable river; today, it is a traffic-clogged visitor attraction on summer weekends. (Even the M25 touches the parish's western boundary, mercifully unseen but sometimes heard). In 1830, Shoreham *having no high road of any public description is but little frequented by travellers and the Turnpike road* [present A225] *being wholly chalk and stones, is by no means pleasant for travelling'*. But with the advent of the railway in 1862 – *'London is only 20 miles away.... a distance now disposed of by a few puffs of steam'* complained Samuel Palmer's son. By 1899 George Spender, at The George, was providing *'good accommodation for cyclists'*; fifty years later, the cyclists came in their *'hundreds...*

in shorts and black alpaca coats, with their haversacks and their bright club stockings'. If cars are substituted for cycles, the millennium has arrived.

It took almost one hundred and fifty years for the whole parish to double its population, from the first Census figures of 828 in 1801. By 1991, the total population had reached 2023. In the 19th century, one new road was laid out: Crown Road; in the century just past, four new roads for Council housing were constructed: in the 1920s Mesne Way and Bowers Road, in the 1950s Forge Way and in the 1960s Palmer's Orchard. After 1945 Bowers Road was given the addition of Mildmay Place. In the 1960s private housing covered the demolished home of the Mildmay squires at Shoreham Place and the low-lying meadow beside the original course of the Darent was developed as Boakes Meadow, named after its former owner.

This booklet takes its beginning at the oldest building in every ancient village – the parish church – in the case of Shoreham having an equally ancient dedication, to St Peter and St Paul. Ken Wilson's interpretation of the late 18th century drawing clearly shows the east window as a small segment together with another small south-east window above the priest's door. The rebuilt 18th century west tower of knapped flint and brick quoins is topped with a spirelet. The modern photograph shows no spirelet but, most significantly, large windows now light the east end and the Mildmay chapel. Also, the priest's door has gone. Much more drastic alterations were made to the interior.

Vincent Perronet, vicar for 57 years from 1728 to 1785, surely appreciated the interior arrangement of the nave: all the box pews faced towards the north where in the middle of the north wall was placed the great three-decker pulpit. The chancel and altar behind the c.1500 rood screen were largely neglected. The Wesley brothers, frequent visitors to the vicarage and good friends of the vicar, would have approved of the church plan. By the time that the first Methodist chapel was built a new spirituality was changing the Established Church. One of the manifestations of the new ideas was the re-discovering and glorifying of the chancel and altar. Thus the windows at the east end were greatly enlarged, the nave seating was re-ordered; new bench pews faced the altar, the fine pulpit was replaced, in accordance with ecclesiological thinking, by the present small pulpit from Westminster Abbey on the left in front of the screen, while the lectern was positioned to its right. The vicarage which Mr Perronet and the Wesleys knew was given large wings on either side to accommodate the large families of vicars at that time.

As for the village itself its plan, until the early 19th century, would in one respect be unfamiliar to today's inhabitants. It would be expected that the earliest settlement would be close to the church and until the advent of a new squire in the person of Sir Walter Stirling, at the turn of the 19th century, there was a warren of cottages between The George and his New Place. 'There were many dangerous turnings, so narrow that carriages could not pass between the houses and gardens'. Sir Walter had them demolished and planned also to buy up and take down the cottages beside the bridge. The truncated appearance of Rising Sun Cottage is evidence of this attempt which ultimately failed. He proposed to construct a sixty-foot wide "new cut" from the Otford-Eynsford road to the Darent bridge, but fortunately the Shoreham Turnpike Act was repealed in 1811 on the grounds that it would provide "no utility" to the village. Thus Shoreham narrowly avoided an earlier version of the M25.

In 1800 the road through the village as far as the church was named Shoreham Street on all land transfers. By the early years of the last century, the High Street covered the same ground as it does today, while the slope down to the river was named School Hill, and the area between the bridge and The George was called Church Road and Church Corner. Today Church Street follows on from the High Street, from the almshouse corner to the church.

Photographs show clearly how little parts of the village have changed in the last hundred years. In Church Street itself, on the right hand side, Ivy Cottage remains as a good example of a late, perhaps cheaply built Wealden hall house and Record retains its fine shop-front from earlier days. William Lambarde in his *Perambulation of Kent* notes that one of the few Kentish bridges in Tudor times was to be found in Shoreham: it may have been near Ark Cottage, over the Manor Drain, which was the original course of the Darent.

After the bridge the land rises again until 'Shoreham Cross' (the present 'T' junction) is reached. On the right, along the High Street, is the other portion of the early village, well above any risk of flooding and with convenient wells in the cottage gardens with Holly Place and Walnut Tree Cottages as good examples of early village buildings.

Introduction

Over the bridge, on the left in Church Street, the new squire, Mr Humphrey St John Mildmay, built a schoolhouse in 1840 at his own expense. A college friend from Cambridge recommended the young Robert Barton, just out of his apprenticeship to a baker, to be the first schoolmaster. In Shoreham he married Sarah Green, from Preston Farm, and she taught the girls sewing and needlework. Sixteen years later the couple left as free emigrants for Australia; their descendants return at regular intervals to maintain their links with the village. The schoolmasters who followed them struggled to keep the children in school away from fruit-picking, hop-picking and working in the brick-field. Epidemics were frequent – typhoid, diphtheria and small-pox were added to the usual infections. At the beginning of the last century the head-master, John Vincent Steane, wished to include rifle shooting in the curriculum: the Board of Education opined that *'it is not a subject (to) be taught to children'*.

Today there are often complaints that there are two Bank holidays in May but by strange coincidence, before the advent of the latter, there were two Shoreham holidays on virtually the same days. The first was on May Day, May 1st, and was called 'Fair Day' held since early times for 'Pedlary' and toys. Possibly the ground used was the Town Field, later the allotments, the old common land of the village; the school log book records that donkey races took place at the Fair. The second Bank holiday was the Village Club Festival of the Shoreham Amicable Benefit Society, held on May 31st, only dating from the 19th century and perhaps centering on the Society's offices in the Walnut Tree property.

Between the school and the almshouses, well back from the street, stands The Terrace. Sale particulars of 1873 suggested that the site was 'admirably adapted' for the building of a tavern and shops. In fact Mr H.B.Mildmay demolished the old buildings and built the present Terrace in 1881. A tavern, The Royal Oak, was built almost opposite on the site of the former parish workhouse and a shop was opened as 'Bell's Stores' at the present No. 1, High Street. Looking down Church Street, in the opposite direction, the large medieval Reedbeds, now The Samuel Palmer School of Art, contains a rarely surviving detached kitchen of the same date as the house.

Returning to Shoreham Cross and the High Street, the early photograph shows no Village Hall (which was built after World War I) while another more recent picture shows the second, and much larger, Wesleyan Methodist chapel which was built in 1878 on the right hand side of the street. This building indicates how greatly the non-conformist congregation had increased during the 19th century – the first Methodist chapel (behind Rising Sun Cottage), built in 1836, could have held only a handful of worshippers. Workers, attracted to the village by the thriving paper mill, and for whom Crown Road was constructed in the 1870's were provided with their own Baptist chapel built at that time.

By the 19th century, the High Street had become the centre of village life with its three shops, three forges and the paper mill at its north end. Humphrey Mildmay had rebuilt three sets of cottages on the western side in the 1830s; his younger son gave the allotments on the old Town Field to the village. The last forge is closed: Miss Dorothy Brown, last surviving child of the last blacksmith, Isaac Brown, lived in the Forge Cottage until the

1980s. Opposite, the one remaining shop, the Village Stores, continues to serve the village. Until the years following World War II, six pubs were spaced at easy walking distance between each other. The three oldest were managed by licensed victuallers (who could sell wine and spirits) – The George, The King's Arms and The Crown; the others, The Rising Sun, The Royal Oak and The Two Brewers were classed as beer-houses, licensed only to sell beer in 1911.

This account has concentrated on people and places; how the villagers earned their daily bread has not been discussed nor the poverty which still stalked the parish. From the late 19th century to the 1920s a soup kitchen operated from the Vicarage each day at 12.30 pm, as the school children and their elders were advised. From Anglo-Saxon times agriculture provided the chief means of employment for the villagers. The early limit of cultivation up the hill above the Recreation Ground can be seen as a line of bushes in the two photographs showing the Cross; the oxen would turn at this point eventually creating this plough bank. The wool the sheep produced was treated at the fulling mill at the Home Farm. Later hops and fruit added to the variety of produce which the valley could support. From the 13th century, the four large farms – Sepham and Filston on the south and Preston and Castle Farm on the north of the village – thrived. Filston, following the fashion, was moated; Castle Farm was, in its beginnings, a small true castle but it was in ruins by Henry VIII's reign and farm buildings arose from the remains – it was still called *The manor of Shoreham Castle* in the 18th century.

In the late 17th century one of the ancient village corn-mills was adapted for the making of hand-made rag paper and as a result, provided an alternative source of employment both for the local population and for paper-makers from other counties until after World War I. By the 19th century its then owner, George Wilmot, was able to build himself a prestigious new house, The Mount, a short distance away from the noise of the mill at work. The Census of 1911 notes the variety of occupations within the mill – the vatmen and couchers who produced the sheets of paper, even an engineer, all male, and the unskilled women workers who carried out the dangerous task of rag-cutting. John Bowers, who gave his name to Bowers Road, was a sizer in the mill.

In 1823 Alexander Baring, about to be created Lord Ashburton, gradually bought up the major part of Shoreham as his daughter Ann's wedding portion when she married Humphrey Mildmay. Near the site of the earlier New Place the Mildmays had a new house built c.1830, Shoreham Place, *'far from beautiful...of yellow brick (with) a roof of purplish slate'* as the Hon. Helen Mildmay later described it. The Mildmays were the titular, if not the legally recognised squires of Shoreham until the untimely death in 1950 of the second Lord Mildmay in a swimming accident near his Devon estate. In the 1950s the house stood deserted and forlorn, with its windows smashed and slates peeling off. It was demolished for the modern Shoreham Place development in the early 1960s. By then, the age-old labour intensive system of agriculture had given way to the modern machine-based industry of the 20th and 21st century, a process which had been greatly hastened by the nation's food requirements in World War II. Coincidentally the death of the second Lord Mildmay seemed to mark a new era which had begun in the countryside.

Ken Wilson has based his view of the church in the late 18th century upon a drawing in the archives of the Kent Archaeological Society. Note the tiny half-circle east window and the spirelet on the west tower as rebuilt in 1775.

A recent photograph shows the tower without its spirelet and the great increase in the size of the east window after 19th century restoration work. *(Garry Weaser)*

The pub, one of the oldest in the village, dating from the 15th century, as it was c. 1900, showing how the road was forced to make a sharp right angle turn around it to reach the bridge over the river. It was one of the three local pubs licensed to sell wines and spirits as well as beer, according to the 1911 Census.

The George is very little changed today, except that the protruding dragon beam on its corner has been seriously damaged by passing articulated lorries attempting to turn the sharp corner. Part of its external timber framing remains intact. *(Garry Weaser)*

Shoreham's link with the expanding Victorian railway system came on 2nd June 1862 when the London, Chatham and Dover Company reached the village from Swanley on its way to Bat and Ball, Sevenoaks. The photograph shows the old booking office and goods shed on the down side.

When the line was electrified in the mid-1930s, it was necessary to build a foot-bridge because of the danger from the third rail to passengers crossing the line. Today the station is un-manned, the goods shed is in private hands and the signal-box has been demolished, but a reasonable train service remains. *(Garry Weaser)*

SHOREHAM PLACE

The home of the Mildmay family for four generations, from c.1830 to 1950, the house was built in Tudorbethan style – *'Far from beautiful . . .. of yellow brick and having a roof of purplish slate'* – it replaced John Borrett's 18th century Palladian villa. By 1955, it was *'deserted and forlorn, with its windows smashed and its slates peeling off . . . a sad decaying house'* and was demolished soon afterwards.

Part of the present Shoreham Place estate, a grouping of detached, semi-detached and terraced New England style houses, built in the early 1960s on the site of the Mildmay house, of which nothing now remains. *(Garry Weaser)*

One of the most interesting buildings in the village as it was c.1900. It was a late Wealden hall house, built angle-on to the road which its solar backs onto, its large external chimney was a later addition. Samuel Palmer painted it as "The Old Cottage" and, more recently, it advertised teas for cyclists.   *(Ian Harper)*

For many years, Ivy Cottage was divided into two units, now it has been restored internally. Its mathematical tiles on its east external wall should be noticed and also its timber-framing on its west wall. *(Garry Weaser)*

Part of its interior dates back to the 16th century, but its present exterior, although without the shop-front, was re-built in 1738. Its name derives from an early 17th century owner named Rickord or Record and a century later, William Pinnocke was dealing in a variety of materials as well as groceries and hardware.

Today, Record has again become a private house but fortunately it has retained its fine 19th century shop-front to what were two shops under the same ownership. The earlier owners, the Lovelands were followed later in the 1930s by the Kingsbury family and it passed into private ownership in 1952. *(Garry Weaser)*

The solid 18th century construction of the main village bridge over the Darent can clearly be seen in this illustration. One of the several public dipping places can be seen on the left. Samuel Palmer made a fine painting of the other side of the bridge as he saw it from Water House. *(Ian Harper)*

Today, the main change in the bridge's appearance is the replacement of the top brick courses on one side by railings. On the far side, the ford can still be used when the river is low. *(Garry Weaser)*

Memorial Cross, Hills & Church, Shoreham, Kent.

It was cut into the chalk on the west slope of the Downs in 1920 as a memorial to the Shoreham dead of World War I. It is one of two Crosses in Kent, the other is outside Lenham, but ours was the first to be made and dedicated.

The same view almost a century later and, apart from the trees which have grown up, a timeless view. Today it commemorates both men and women of the village who have given their lives in the two World Wars. *(Garry Weaser)*

Externally it appears to date from the 17th to 18th centuries and certainly it was called The King's Head until Victorian times. It is the second village pub whose higher status gave it the right to sell wines and spirits as well as the humbler beer. *(Garry Weaser)*

Like The George its present view hardly differs from its earlier one. Also, both pubs share in the considerable re-arrangement of their bar areas to cater for present day customers. *(Garry Weaser)*

High Street, Shoreham.

A 19th century view of what was still called first Shoreham Street then High Street, looking down past the 1840s village School on the right and on towards the river. What was then an open sewer on the right hand side of the road still remains as part of the local drainage system.

Now enveloped in tall trees, The Samuel Palmer School of Art on the left often confuses visitors. Equally, its name – Reedbeds – could deceive, as it only dates from the last century, its earliest name being Balsattes. Samuel Palmer did not live there, he leased it in his later years when he became affluent. But the house was, in the Middle Ages, one of the finest timber framed buildings in the village, and beside it still remains its ancient detached kitchen. *(Garry Weaser)*

This view of the village school, showing its schoolmaster's house attached to the school room just as it was built in 1840-1, faces onto Church Street. Robert Barton, its first headmaster, would have recognised the exterior view, but not the present interior which now houses the school office, common room and extensions. *(Garry Weaser)*

The school seen from its playground – the opposite view of the building seen on the left. New development, providing extra classroom facilities on the rear of the building, has not altered its frontage which remains as Mr. Mildmay built it. *(Garry Weaser)*

In 1964, Franklin White of Reedbeds copied an old picture of a substantial, then sub-divided, building fronting Church Street and adjacent to the village cage (lockup). In 1873. Mr. H.B. Mildmay bought the *'four freehold Brick and timber built cottages'*, demolished them and built the present Terrace in 1881. *(Franklin White)*

The present Terrace whose site was described in its sale particulars as *'admirably adapted'* for the building of a tavern and shops. The tavern was built almost opposite as The Royal Oak, and the shop, utilising an existing building, was the former Central Mart in the High Street. *(Garry Weaser)*

As seen just before their recent restoration and looking much the same as when they were first built in the late 15th century and justly described as *'one of the architectural gems of the village'*. In 1473, John Roos or Rose of Filston endowed them for three poor men or women together with alms of 7d per week each. *(Philip Rogers)*

As they are today. the three have been made into two fully modernised dwellings, as a memorial by the family of *'a young airman, Dudley Greenwood'* of Coombe Hollow, Shoreham, who was reported missing in action in 1943. *(GarryWeaser)*

This c.1900 photograph looks north from Shoreham Cross (roads) up Shoreham Street, as it was still known at this date. The buildings on the right, which include the former Royal Oak beer-house, were built in the 1870s, on the land and site of the former parish work-house, sold in 1847.

The same view photographed recently showing how the Royal Oak, which closed as a pub in August 2000, has re-invented itself as a private house. The small building just beyond, was, for many years, one of the dozen or so village shops, and is now the thriving Honeypot Tea Rooms. *(Garry Weaser)*

As one house, it was known as Oxbourne Farm when, in the 18th century, it was owned by a member of the Waring family of Chelsfield. The fire mark of Thomas Waring's Sun Insurance Office policy is attached to the front wall. For much of the last century it was one of the chief grocery shops in the village – the Central Mart, owned by the Bell brothers.

Now divided into two units and with the name of Oxbourne having migrated to Mill Lane, the front room of No. 1, High Street has had bow windows put in place of the former shop front. Lilac Cottage on the left, like several other sub-divided buildings in the village, has a flying-freehold upper room extending over its neighbour. *(Garry Weaser)*.

By 1878 the small Methodist chapel built in 1836 in Chapel Alley was too small for the growing congregation, so in that year this fine building was constructed in the High Street opposite the Landway. *(Sevenoaks Methodist Circuit)*

By the 1960s, the numbers attending the Methodist chapel had dwindled to single figures and sadly the decision was taken to demolish it and replace it with these semi-detached houses. Today it might have been preserved and adapted by a private owner. *(Garry Weaser)*

E.M. Bilbrough

Old house Shoreham, Kent.

The north wing of one of the finest surviving village yeoman houses is of 15th century date, with its major portion being rebuilt a century later on the probable site of an open medieval hall. In 1823, now known as Round's Place, it acted as the farmhouse for William Round. The illustration shows the 'dwelling house with butcher's shop, built of plaster, timber and tiles' when it was let to Frederick Boakes in 1894.

Holly Place today as seen from Duncan Wood's house opposite. The present owners have themselves removed the exterior plaster to reveal the timber-framing and original windows on the north wing and the brickwork of the 16th century re-construction of the main building. *(Garry Weaser)*

Townfield Cottages probably started life as squatters homes before being rebuilt more permanently. They stood until World War II, when they were destroyed by a delayed action high explosive bomb, almost opposite Orchard House on a site now occupied by several bungalows.

The same view today. The name of Townfield Cottages reminds us that they stood on the ancient village common field, now the allotments, which Mr. Mildmay gave to villagers in the 1870s in order that they could grow their own vegetables. *(Garry Weaser)*

The 16th century Forge Cottage, built, like several others in Shoreham, angle-on to the road, is of timber-frame construction and contains many original features. Our drawing shows it's attachment to the Forge itself. The latter, although now a garage, still contains much of its old equipment which the Browns would have made to suit their individual needs.

The Forge and its adjoining cottage have both remained remarkably unchanged for well over a century. Miss Brown, the last surviving member of the family, lived in the un-modernised Forge Cottage until her death in the 1980s. *(Garry Weaser)*

Blacksmith Reuben Brown, who moved his family from Meadow Cottage, was followed as blacksmith and farrier by his sons Solomon and Isaac; they were all devout non-conformists. After Isaac's death in 1935, the forge continued to be used by several smiths until the middle of the last century *(Peter Batley)*

The only remaining one of the three forges which, until the 19th century, dominated this section of the High Street. The Brown family of smiths had at first been established in Meadow Cottage beside the river (destroyed in World War II), moving to the High Street in 1860. *(Garry Weaser)*

In 1921, the first Co-operative store opened in Shoreham and this photograph shows the first assistant, Amy McLening (later Amy Higgins), with the manager standing beside her in the doorway. Shortly afterwards, the South Suburban Co-op. Society took it over and it remained as one of the larger village stores until its closure in February 1980. *(Amy Higgins)*

After its closure the shop struggled under several owners, but by 2010 it had finally closed its doors and is about to be demolished, giving a frontage for the former manager's house which stands behind it. *(Garry Weaser)*

This shows the third of the village pubs licensed to sell wines and spirits as well as beer. Like The George, it is medieval in date, but possibly the older of the two since it was constructed angle-on to the High Street. The interior has seen much re-construction and the earliest part to be seen today dates from the fifteenth century.

Today the exterior is little changed, although the malt-house is closed, except for the small extension on the right hand side and for the construction of Crown Road beside it on the line of a former foot-path. *(Garry Weaser)*

This was the first new road to be built in the village for many centuries and it indicates the importance of papermaking to the community. Skilled paper-makers were itinerant, moving to whichever mill could provide employment. Under George Wilmot's ownership in the19th century Shoreham's mill thrived, hence the building of Crown Road for its workmen in the 1860s and 70s.

The closely packed houses appear little changed as far as their exteriors are concerned, but they no longer house any paper-makers, rather new-comers to the village getting a first foot-hold in local property. This explains the cars parked end to end on both sides of the road. At the far end, on the right, the artist Harold Copping had his studio and home. *(Garry Weaser)*

The Mill

THE MILL, SHOREHAM.

The surviving complex of timber buildings housing the varied processes required to make rag paper were of 19th century date, at which time steam power was installed to supplement any lack of water power. The coming of the railway in 1862 made the transport of the finished paper much simpler. George Wilmot forsook his 1690s house, building a quieter home on his own land a short distance away, which he called The Mount.

The Mill House was rebuilt in the 1690s at the time when rag paper began to be made in its workshops. It is a good example of late 17th century vernacular architecture. Since 1936, when the mill buildings were demolished, the architecture of the house and its position, surrounded by two channels of the river Darent, can be truly appreciated. Close by a Roman bath block was excavated a few years ago, possibly indicating a site of a Roman villa. *(James Saynor)*

An early photograph looking down Mill Lane, then un-made, to the mill, taken in the 1920s. The Domesday corn-mill had been converted to making rag paper in the 1690s using the water power supplied by the Darent, and was still in production at this date. *(Desmond Draffin)*

Today the mill has been closed for some 80 years and the mill buildings were demolished in 1936, leaving the fine Mill House of the late 17th century. The iron mill wheel, beside the leat, survived until the 1940s when it was taken away to supply war needs. *(Garry Weaser)*

REMAINS OF SHORAM CASTLE.

It was still called "Shoreham Castle" in the Darenth (sic) Valley Main Sewerage Award of 1881, when it had an acreage of 321 acres. Although a small castle in the 13th century, by Henry VIII's reign it was in ruins and in 1847, *'scarcely any part is now visible, a farm house having been built out of the ruins'*. (Sevenoaks Library, Local Studies Collection)

Today the enterprising farm owners, the Alexander family, who first settled in Eynsford after leaving Scotland in 1892 with their 20 cows and a bull, have filled their fields with crops of lavender while continuing to follow traditional farming methods. The farm house itself is an excellent example of more than four hundred years of preserved timber framed architecture. *(Garry Weaser)*

Acknowledgements

Allen Grove Fund, Kent Archaeological Society

Sevenoaks Library, Local Studies Collection

Caroline Alexander

Meg Chapman

Desmond Draffin

Ian Harper for the frontispiece and for copying old photographs

Ken Wilson

Robin Wood, whom we would particularly wish to thank for his allowing us to make use of his invaluable collection of historic postcards.

Bibliography

Bagshaw, S. *History, Gazetteer and Directory . Kent* (1847)

Ireland, W.H. *History of the County of Kent* (1830)

Kelly's Post Office Directory of Kent for 1878 and 1899.

"London Calling". B.B.C. World Service (1944)

Mildmay Papers, Sales Particulars for "the Terrace" 1873

Mitchell, V. and Smith, K. *Swanley to Ashford* (1995).

Payne, Augustus, *History of the Parish Church ... Shoreham* (A. Payne, 1930).

Rogers, Philip, *A Vale in Kent* (1955)

White, M and Saynor, J. *Shoreham, A Village in Kent* (1989)

Index

Map Key